THIS IS YOUR WAKE-UP CALL
LIVE YOUR DREAMS
DR. TODD M. HALL

THIS IS YOUR WAKE-UP CALL
LIVE YOUR DREAMS
DR. TODD M. HALL

Sovereign King's Creation, LLC.
Mobile, Alabama

Published by Sovereign King's Creation, LLC
P.O. Box 161367
Mobile, Alabama 36616
www.sovereignkingscreation.com

First printing, February 2007

Printed in the United States of America

First published by Sovereign King's Creation, LLC

ISBN: 978-0-9793-978-0-6

Layout and Cover design: Florence Edi

All Scripture is taken from The King James Version of the Bible.

CONTENTS

DEDICATION

To the eternal Dream Giver, Dream Fulfiller, Jesus—Your Kingdom shall last forever.

To the millions who in this season will hear and answer the divine call of God for their lives—may this book serve as God's trumpet in your soul which propels you to awake and live your dreams.

To the young at heart—seasons may have passed, but there remains a dream awaiting your participation.

To the young in age—you are never too young to realize your dreams. However, be wise in your speech as you are prompted to ask what you will.

FOREWORD

Greetings Child of God,

You are now holding one of the most powerful tools in the kingdom of God's end-time arsenal. There has been an unprecedented onslaught of attack from the enemy's camp against the dream manifestation of the Saints of the Most High God. This attack has caused many in the body of Christ to lay comatose in a bed of unfulfilled dreams. This comatose state has produced limp Christians—those who fail to dream or those who fail to awake from their dreams.

Dr. Todd Hall, in this timely book, *This Is Your Wake-up Call: Live Your Dreams,* encourages and ignites the believer to arise, take up his/her bed and walk out the dream. He encourages you to carefully examine the pages of this book as you read about the dream manifestation of Adam, Joseph and Solomon. As God was with these great men of God, so He is with you.

While you meditate on Section one, Adam and a Dream Comes True, you will be reminded that God not only feels your infirmities, but He has already supplied within you the answer to any infirmity, void, or lack in your life. Just as God reached into Adam and pulled out Eve, know that as you digest this book, the Creator God Himself is reaching into you and pulling out your manifestation. He may put you to sleep for a short period of time to get what is in you out, but understand that there is an appointed time and season for you to awake and not only embrace your manifestation, but to subdue the earth with your manifestation.

Moreover, you may be one who has been lied on, cheated, talked about, and mistreated. The Joseph section of this prophetic manual will empower you to go through the storm to secure the manifestation of your prophetic encounter. You will cease to abhor your suffering for righteousness sake, because you will realize that you are truly in the company of Jesus and that you are on your way to dream fulfillment.

Last, but not least, truly Solomon was the son of King David. However, you are the sons and daughters of the King of kings. If God answered Solomon's request according to Solomon's words, then imagine what God will do for you in whom the Blood covers and the Holy Spirit resides. God is demonstrating that you are an heir who is able to make your request known—even in your sleep—and when you awake you will have what you asked.

Do not allow your God-given dreams to be sifted as wheat. Know that *This Is Your Wake-up Call: Live Your Dreams.*

Arneece L. Williams, J.D.
Legacy Builders, Sovereign King's Creation
Mobile, Alabama

All thought and revelation are based upon personal experiences and angles by which the author sees life.

INTRODUCTION

Reality of Sleep State

Here begins the reading of God's Holy Word. May He sancti-fy it in our hearts that it may be used again to help somebody as we travel along the way.

Notice that most of your dreams, visions and ambitions do not come until you have gone through a night experience. We see that in Gibeon, the Lord appeared to Solomon in a dream by night. We could really stay in this one phrase for an hour.

I Kings 3:5 In Gibeon the Lord appeared to Solomon in a dream by night...

There is something about the night. Folk do not dream well in the daytime. There is something about the sun and the day that keeps you awake, but the feeling and the season of night allows you to sleep. Can I teach? I don't know what happens to you at night. It seems as if your metabolic rate slows down and if you eat then you really get it. All of your organs, your kidneys, liver, and heart-beat slow down and sleep. While your body is sleeping the power leaves the organs that kept you awake all day and gives authority to your mind and says, "You take it from here." Oh, did you hear that? Oh yes, your mind can function like that. As a matter of fact, your mind can remember things that have happened to you, whether consciously or sub-consciously, where this recalling caus-es your physical body to react. This happens the other way around as well. Memories can cause you to have a dream or a nightmare. Oh, I'm not deep enough yet. Maybe I need to go deeper.

It is important that you catch that God is even with you in your sleep. Okay, I will prove it. Watch this. Have you ever had a semi-nightmare where you were running fast from a dog, but the thing is catching up with you? You were running in slow motion, although you were giving it all that you had—that is if you have ever been through anything in your sleep. It is funny that when the very thing that wants to kill you gets ready to get you, you wake-up breathing hard. Now, I ask, "Who woke your happy self up? Why is it that the thing that is after you in your sleep never catches you?" I hear you deep folk saying, "Umm, that is something to give thought to."

Most of your dreams, visions and ambitions do not come until you have gone through a night experience.

Have you ever had a deep sleep where you were having a semi-nightmare of falling off of something and just before you hit the bottom you woke up out of breath? Well, who woke you up? Today, there is more scientific proof that those who die in their sleep without a cause may have been having a dream from which they could not wake-up. Hence, the thing in the dream that was after them caught them. So, the doctor would call it death by natural causes because he was not in the dream. Then the doctor who saw him for an annual check-up the day before would say, "There was nothing wrong with his heart; there was nothing wrong with him. He was perfect when he came here yesterday. He just died." After the doctors would be unable to explain the death, they would chalk it up to natural causes. In fact, the cause of death is that you gave the enemy access to your dream and he killed you in your sleep.

There is one thing that you cannot give outsiders access to—your dream. Oh, you did not like what I said. I repeat. Do not give outsiders access to your dream. If you let somebody into your dream, they may try to kill you in your sleep. Be mindful that there are certain things that God is revealing to you that you cannot tell certain folk. I hope that I am not boring you, but dream state is so powerful. It is so powerful that you can go to sleep and dream that you are walking, then while you are having that dream you actually get up and start walking while still asleep. Such actions have been recorded and studied. Scientists attach things to people and tape them in their sleep; they are known as sleep walkers. They get up and start walking.

The same thing has occurred with talking while sleeping. Some of you have been busted by the enemy and even a loved one because you talk in your sleep. You revealed your weakness in your sleep. Brenda asked while you were sleeping, "Who are you dreaming about?" You answered, "Sally." When you woke up, Brenda was looking at you funny asking, "Who is Sally?" Busted! Sleep can get you! A dream can get you in trouble when you awake. Women are experts at that, "What are you dreaming about? Where is the wallet? Were you really at work yesterday?"

The cause of death is that you gave the enemy access to your dream and he killed you in your sleep.

You have sleep walkers and sleep talkers. Both are in dream state, dreaming something that is making their natural organs expressive. So, whoever is around you is seeing and hearing outwardly an event or conversation that is taking place inwardly.

You may be saying, "I'm not concerned about a nightmare or what others may hear me say in my sleep or about my dreams. I have God with me and types of sleep state are not that important, be it a dream or a nightmare." On that note, enter in and let me show you the significance of dreams.

SECTION ONE

ADAM AND A DREAM COMES TRUE

There is a dream inside of you that is awaiting its birth.
-Dr. Todd M. Hall

Although you may feel groggy at times because you are experiencing your cycles of sleep that are congruent to anesthesia, I implore you to become enthused about receiving your dream manifestation. As you feast on *Adam and a Dream Comes True*, see yourself on the table of your garden, being prepped by the Master Surgeon to undergo a surgical procedure that will birth divine increase in your life.

1

Deep Sleep

Genesis 2:21-22 And the Lord God caused a deep sleep to fall upon Adam, and he slept and he took one of his ribs, and closed up the flesh instead thereof.

Verse 22 And the rib, which the Lord God had taken from man, made he a woman, and brought her unto the man.

The book of Genesis records that God placed Adam in a deep sleep and when Adam awoke the fulfillment of his need was looking him in the face. Allow me to give you some background before we dissect Genesis 2:21-22.

Adam served God everyday, at the cool of the day *(Genesis 3:8)*, which means towards the evening when the sun is going down. Do not miss it. God met him towards the night, because nighttime typifies romance. I am sorry that you missed that. Of course romance can occur during the day hours, but it is not the same as nightfall. Oh, I can tell when folk are home alone and are not dreaming at all. Adam and God met each other everyday on schedule. They fellowshipped and talked. We do not know what they spoke about daily because the scripture does not record the conversation. It is not written because certain things are between you and God. It was so deep that he did not even invite Eve. We see that Eve was somewhere talking to the devil, while Adam is somewhere hanging out with God. Did you catch that? Come with me up here. I am not coming down.

I am flying because you need to know how other folk who hang with you can get jealous of you when you are telling them your dream. You are hanging out with God and they are not in the dream. They are spending time hearing what the enemy is saying. The enemy is telling them that you think that you are somebody and that you are trying to act as if you are better than everyone else. If they would just get a dream, they would not be jealous. Tell your enemy to go somewhere and dream! I have seen husbands and wives get jealous of each other. One says that the other one is always going to church. If both of you are saved, who can get jealous of a God who put you together? That is a reflection that somebody is not dreaming.

If I get married and my future wife says, "Do you have to go do another revival?" I know something is wrong with her. I would have to say to her, "I have you because of all the time that I gave God. I spent time with God; then He sent you." Let me show you this in the scriptures. Adam keeps going to God when he is single. Notice that Adam is single, yet whole. He is whole, but he is single. You do not have to get married to be whole, because you are whole before you get married. Okay, I will leave that alone. If you are not whole and the person that you marry makes you whole, then when he/she leaves you are no longer whole.

Certain things are between you and God.

The Bible says that Adam kept going to God, romancing God at night. Adam kept going to God, romancing Him spirit to Spirit. However, Adam is flesh and God cannot please his flesh. That which is of flesh is flesh and that which is of spirit is spirit. So, God and Adam romance spiritually. The dialogue went something like this: "Lord, I thank you!" "Adam, I bless you." "Lord, you are great!" "Adam, I know it." "Lord, without you I am nothing!" "You had better believe it." "God you have given me all of this." "Yes, I have." "God you are the only one that I love." "I'd better be." It is all spiritual. Notice that Adam never mentions one time that he is lonely. Adam never declares himself to be lonely. Preachers need to stop preaching that error. Tell every pastor that said that NOT TO PREACH IT ANYMORE! The Bible said that God knew that Adam was lonely. Genesis 2:18 records that God said, *"It is not good for man to be alone; I will make him an help meet for him."* Adam did not tell God because when you are in love with somebody and you are in covenant, you can feel when something is wrong.

While God had taken note that Adam was lonely, Adam continued to go to God for fellowship. God had Adam naming animals and everything. The whole time, God had Adam on His mind. He was checking out the animals that He had brought to Adam and noticed that *"there was not found a help meet for [Adam]."* (Genesis 2:20) Then God looked at Adam and made him sleep. Here we are again, witnessing God producing something while you sleep. As a matter of fact, the scripture says that God made Adam to fall into a *deep sleep. (Genesis 2:21)*

Tell your enemy to go somewhere and dream!

According to scientific studies, deep sleep is the stage of sleep that precedes the rapid eye movement (REM) stage, which is the stage where dreams are produced and rehearsed. In the normal functioning of things, there are other stages of sleep that precedes deep sleep. However, we see here that God fast forwarded Adam's sleep pattern and began him in deep sleep. Why did He do this?

God is doing a fast forward in your sleep! It is not until you have a dream that you receive the vision that God has for your life. You receive it in your sleep and not just any part of sleep state—but in your dreams, which occurs directly after deep sleep. Say out loud, "God is doing a fast forward in my sleep!"

Adam romanced God daily and it prompted God to skip Adam over some natural stages. So, when you get what you have dreamed and the haters attack you for it, because in their finite minds they cannot reconcile your time of stepping on the scene to your manifestation, just tell them that you and God had a thing going on.

God put Adam into a deep sleep and pulled out of him what he did not ask. They would not know that you and God had been romancing one another in the cool of the day, while they were out hanging with satan—trying to get their needs met without touching the very heart of God! They were busy seeking things, instead of seeking God. So, because Adam mastered how to touch God, God put Adam into a deep sleep and pulled out of him what he did not ask.

As previously mentioned, God caused Adam to go into a deep sleep. He had to go into a deep sleep because he was about to undergo surgery. So, he had to be put under. God says that if you are not in a deep sleep to get what I am going to give to you, you will feel the pain. God wants you to get this without pain. Child of God, do not miss this. Adam is just laying there, in his God sleep, which is the best kind of sleep. When you are in a God sleep, you only dream about your destiny. You only dream about your new anointing. You only dream about how many of your relatives are going to get saved. When it is a God sleep, it is all good. You do not see any devils. You do not have any flashbacks. You do not wake–up out of breath. You get up with a smile on your face, a dance in your feet and clapping in your hands. God knows.

2

Adam and a Dream Comes True

It is remarkable that while Adam is in this deep sleep that God reaches into his side and performs surgery with His very own hands. This is a surgery that only God can do. God pulls out a rib from Adam's rib cage. The number one job of the rib cage is to protect the vital organs of the body. So, he is not giving Adam just any old woman, but he is giving him a woman that has his back. God reaches into Adam's side, pulls out a rib and fashions the rib. It is remarkable because the second job of a rib cage, which is attached to the back vertebrae, is to make sure men walk straight. So, God is giving Adam a woman to make sure that he does not get out of order and that he remains in the place of God that he should be. Therefore, you do not have your dream woman or dream man unless that person has your back and will make sure that you and God stay tight like that. Anything that draws you away from God is a nightmare. Can I get some help? Anything that gets jealous when you give God praise is a demon.

When you are in a God sleep, you only dream about your destiny.

While Adam is sound asleep, God is playing multifaceted roles in the dream. God steps into Adam as God. Then, He goes into Adam's side while He is performing surgery, at which time He is the Surgeon. God places Adam in a deep sleep. Hence, He is also the anesthesiologist. Do you hear me? Then He fashions the woman. Now, He is the in-law of Adam, while He is yet the God and the Father of Adam. God now becomes Mother Nature and makes a woman. Then He becomes the Priest to do the marriage. Every role in the dream is God. You know when God has done a thing for you because all you can say is that God did it. Who woke you up this morning? "God." Who started you on your way? "God." Who put food on your table? "God." Who healed you when you were sick? "God." Who paid your bills when you did not have any money? "God." Well wake up and know that it is real! God is the same yesterday; He is the same today; He is the same forever! *(Hebrews 13:8)*

If you do any study on anatomy or biology, you will realize that it is illegal for man to have more than one wife. The Muslims are out of order. Folks are just out of order, if they believe that you can have one and then get one free. You only gave one rib! You can only get what is missing and Adam is only missing one rib. So, if you believe that you should have six wives, then you need to get rid of a slab. Oh, good God right now! I think that this is too deep. You must look at the system of God. God only replaces what He takes. Can I get a witness?

Anything that draws you away from God is a nightmare.

Men have thirteen ribs and women have fourteen because women came here whole and men came lonely. Did you hear what I have said? A woman can do without a man, but a man cannot do without a woman. Are you getting quiet? That is why systematically the government is on the side of the woman. She gets half even if she does not work. If you give her a baby, she gets child support. This is so because God made her for you. Can I get a witness?

Further in the word of God, God presents Adam's dream to him as reality. When Adam woke-up, what he had dreamed was staring him in the face. Do you know how you feel when you come from under anesthesia? I had arthroscopic knee surgery where they put me under and when I came to I did not know how I arrived where I was. I did not feel them go in. Neither did I feel them stitch it up. All I know is that they put me under and when I woke-up I was somewhere else and I woke-up very slowly. I did not wake-up slowly because I was tired. As a matter of fact, I felt extremely well rested. The Bible states that when Adam awakened from his deep sleep, what he was longing for was standing over him and Adam called her woman. *(Genesis 2:23)*

SECTION TWO

JOSEPH AND A DREAM COMES TRUE

Suffering Seals the Dream.
-Dr. Todd M. Hall

In order to have dream manifestation, you must be able to endure to the end, which takes energy. So, yes, there is a place for sleep because sleep is representative of the restorative process that will give you the energy necessary to battle the devils that will attempt to abort your delivery. As you delve into *Joseph and a Dream Comes True,* fully energized at full throttle, know that God will deliver you into the place where dreams come true. Realize that the place is not somewhere over the rainbow, but it is right where you are today! You are occupying your place of dream manifestation!

3

Giving The Enemy Access To Your Dream

Genesis 37:5 And Joseph dreamed a dream, and he told it his brethren: and they hated him yet the more.

Here, we see that Joseph had a dream. He did not have any money, but he had a dream. We also see that when he told his dream to his brothers they hated him even more. Now, if the devil can hate you for something that you received in your sleep, picture then what he is going to try to do to you when you wake up and go after what you just dreamed.

Notice that Genesis 37:5 reads that Joseph's brothers hated him "yet the more," which means that there was *Joseph did not have any money, but he had a dream.* already some hate there before God started speaking to him in a dream. Allow me to slow walk this as not to miss anything. Allow me to take my time for a moment to lay some ground work. Let's take a look at the verses which precede the above verse, Genesis 37:1-4.

Verse 1   And Jacob dwelt in the land...
Verse 2   These are the generations of Jacob. Joseph being sev-
enteen years old was feeding the flock with his brethren... and Joseph
brought unto his father their evil report.
Verse 3   Now Israel loved Joseph more than all his children,
because he was the son of his old age: and he made him a coat of many
colours.
Verse 4 And when his brethren saw that their father loved him
more than all his brethren, they hated him, and could not speak peace-
ably unto him.

Before going any farther, understand that Jacob is Joseph's natural father, as well as his spiritual father.   Hence, observe the
changes in reference from verse one to verse three— to the natural
father Jacob and the spiritual father Israel. Bearing this in mind,
note that the scripture references the man as Jacob in verses one
and two, then when the word speaks of who loved Joseph more
than all his children, it refers to Israel. Know that Jacob did not
name himself Israel; God named him Israel to represent a kingdom
transformation. So, I submit that when Israel is used to refer to
Jacob, it is representative of the God in him.

Now, following the above notion, imagine God loving Joseph
more than all of His children. Okay, I hear your thoughts. You
are saying, "God is not a respecter of persons. He loves all of us
the same." Well, the Bible says that Mary was highly favored
among women. Highly favored means well-favored, favored above
others, or to look differently upon a person than one does upon
another. God did not go around taking applications on who
would be the special one to carry Jesus; He chose. He directed His
favor more towards one woman than another.

We see that Joseph, the boy, received a coat of many colors and was loved by the father and his brothers hated him. Imagine if these brothers were Mary's sisters when the Holy Ghost moved upon her and imparted the Savior Himself to incubate in her womb for nine months. Mary would not have been able to share her wonderful news with the sisters. Imagine Mary going to the sisters saying, "You know girl, an angel came to me as I was planning my wedding and spoke a message to me saying that I am highly favored among women. Then the Holy Spirit Himself came upon me and now I am pregnant with the Savior. His name will be Jesus. Please, my sisters believe me." "Well, praise the Lord, Mary, we believe you." As soon as Mary would turn her back a sister would say to the other, "Now, girl, you know didn't no Holy Ghost come upon her. She is lying and the truth ain't in her, because if God wanted the Messiah to be birth through this household, He would have used me because I am the oldest. The favor is supposed to come to me and not to her." Don't forget to put that gossipy tone on it.

Simply stated, when you can erase the fact that Mary was highly favored of God to carry and give birth to the Christ, we can dismiss that God could love Joseph more than his brothers. Oh, you cannot erase that fact. Can you?

So, we see that the house of Israel (translation—church folk) hated on a seventeen-year-old child because the Father loved him more and the Father gave him a gift to cover him. This reminds me of the Pharisees, Sadducees, and Jesus. You must know that Joseph is a type of Christ. You don't like that do you? I am moving on.

Evidently, these boys were not doing what Joseph was doing. The word does not reference exactly what Joseph was doing, but we do know that his brothers were murderers, liars, and adulterers.

They broke an oath that their father had made to another nation because of pride and killed all of the men in that community. One brother even slept with his father's wife. They also gave an evil-report, which is what Joseph reported to Jacob in Genesis 37:2. So, maybe if they functioned in some integrity, they could be covered the same way as Joseph.

The fight has never been over you, but over the anointing that is on your life.

Verse four not only indicates that the brethren hated Joseph, but they could not speak peaceably to him. They had no kind words to say to him. They had only harsh words to speak. Come on. You have heard such harsh words as, "You will never amount to anything. You won't get any of daddy's stuff. You were a mistake." Why such a response because he happened to be loved a little more and got a coat? I am glad you asked. That coat represented not only a spiritual covering, but an anointing. Here we go.

The fight has never been over you, but over the anointing that is on your life. The fight is over the word that was spoken before you were in your mother's womb. It has always been over the anointing and the enemy can see it even when you are still broke—even before signs and wonders follow your ministry. The enemy can see it, because verse four states that they *"saw that their father loved him more than all his brethren"*. The enemy can see it sometimes before you realize what is on you. The enemy will hate you for it because he can never wear the anointing again. It has been forever snatched from his reach. He can see something that he can never ever have! All he can do is remember what it felt like. What a torture!

Another reason that we know that an anointing was transferred to Joseph is that after the pressure of being hated, ridiculed and disenfranchised by his brethren, the anointing that was present was made manifest in a prophetic encounter called a dream. In breaking it down, verses 3 and 4 read that Joseph was loved, anointed and hated, then immediately verse 5 reads that Joseph dreamed a dream. Oh, yes.

Genesis 37:5 And Joseph dreamed a dream, and he told it his brethren: and they hated him yet the more.

Stay with me Saints. I told you that we would come back to it, but first we had to get some grounding. Now let's look into the first dream recorded in Genesis 37:6-8.

Verse 6 And he said unto them, Hear, I pray you, this dream which I have dreamed:
Verse 7 For, behold we were binding sheaves in the field, and, lo, my sheaf arose, and also stood upright; and, behold, your sheaves stood round about, and made obeisance to my sheaf.
Verse 8 And his brethren said to him, Shalt thou indeed reign over us? Or shalt thou indeed have dominion over us? And they hated him yet the more for his dreams, and for his words.

Joseph's dream has several representations in it. First of all, the dream takes place in the harvest. How many of you know that we are a part of the harvest? The church is a part of the harvest. Joseph and his brothers are a part of the harvest and out of the harvest arose a standard. Follow me. In the dream Joseph's sheaf was raised from among his brethren. I will keep reminding you that Joseph is indeed a typification of Jesus. Know that I have been commissioned to market Jesus in everything. Jesus was the Prophet who was raised from among His brethren. *(Deuteronomy 18:18)* This is very significant. Do not think that the enemy does not

> *The anointing that was present, was made manifest in prophetic encounter called a dream.*

understand this about your dream. He is trembling just thinking about what you have been commissioned to do. Go ahead and declare, "I have been raised from among my brethren. I do not know exactly where I am going, but I do know that I have been commissioned to do damage to the kingdom of darkness and as I will see later I have been ordained to save a nation." You see, while you are trying to hold on to the place where you currently are, God is raising you up from among them. Yeah, they saw you when you scooted, crawled, walked and fell. Now they get to sit in the VIP section to see you as God raises you up from among them. He is calling you to a place of rulership, reign, and dominion. Tell them to keep talking about you and hating you so that you can have a dream!

It is no secret that you are going to be hated for your dream.

Joseph's sheaf is also indicative of a plumb-line because it stood upright like a wall that is not crooked. Remember my Jesus mantle. God said that He would *"set a plumb-line in the midst of His people Israel." (Amos 7:8)* So, He set a straight place in the midst of liars, thieves, murderers, and adulterers. In other words when people ridicule you for not compromising, you stand upright and direct them to part "b" of Genesis 37:7, which reads ...*and behold your sheaves stood round about, and made obeisance to my sheaf.* Let them deal with your dream, but know that they will hate you for your dream and for your words. *(Genesis 37:8)*

> *Genesis 37:9 And he dreamed yet another dream, and told it his brethren, and said, Behold, I have dreamed a dream more; and, behold, the sun and the moon and the eleven stars made obeisance to me.*
> *Verse 10 And he told it to his father, and to his brethren: and his father rebuked him, and said unto him, What is this dream that thou hast dreamed? Shall I and thy mother and thy brethren indeed*

come to bow down ourselves to thee to the earth?

By now Joseph must already be feeling the tension in the atmosphere because his brothers already have an escalating hate towards him. Let's recap. Joseph was hated because he was loved more than his brethren; he was covered more and he had a dream. Saints, it is no secret that you are going to be hated for your dream. It's no secret that sometimes you are going to be hated by those closest to you.

However, notice that every time Joseph was hated God gave him a dream. This dream is the second dream and this time he tells his brothers and his father. In this dream, Joseph sees that his father, mother and brothers are going to bow themselves to Joseph. What? Could this be God? Take notice that the father rebukes Joseph. Now I don't know which spirit rebuked—Jacob or Israel. Okay do not forget what you have learned so far because I will refer back to it.

To find out who was rebuking, let's walk through this thing without getting ahead of ourselves. If the dream was not from God then it was Israel, the God in Jacob rebuking Joseph. If the dream was from God, then it was Jacob rebuking Joseph. Know that any house divided will fall—it will not stand. So, God would not come against His own Spirit. Because we all have read our Bibles, we know that the dream was true. Therefore, it must not have been Israel rebuking Joseph. It was Jacob. Quite simply put, it was not God rebuking Joseph.

Don't panic. It's okay when someone does not see the God in you or His purpose for your life. Some will desire to nourish the dream. Some will attempt to edit the dream, while others will simply observe. Either way God's word is the last word no matter who does or does not see it. It's clearly shown here that there may be times when some things concerning you may not be revealed to anyone but you and that is okay. Remember that God is the author of promotion. Promotion comes from Him and when He places promotion on you no man can stop it.

You see child of God, it is important to note that God is not obligated to function within the confines of man's ordinances. He will do as it pleases Him and only has to seek His own counsel. He does not have to ask permission. God is God and there is none beside Him. God did not have to start with Reuben, who was the first born or with Judah, Jacob's strength. Instead, he raised up the seventh son, a seventeen year-old boy, to save the world. Joseph did not just save Israel, but the world—Egypt and all of its territories.

Genesis 37:11 And his brethren envied him…

The brethren went from hating to envying Joseph. Now tell me that a dream will not provoke the enemy. Do not do that. I will not be guilty of enticing you to lie. Know that envy is something else; it made the chief priests deliver Jesus for crucifixion. *(Matthew 27:18 and Mark 15:10)* So, know that Joseph is about to suffer something because his brethren—the patriarchs envied him. That is something; the enemy envied a seventeen-year-old child who had a dream. Oh don't be scared…the Christ lives in you.

There may be times when some things concerning you may not be revealed to anyone but you.

4

Vision in Dark Places:
From the Pit to the Palace—Part One

Now it's been established that Joseph was hated and envied because of his dream. Let's view what the hate and envy produced in the life of Joseph.

The word of God records that Joseph's brethren went to feed his father's flock in Shechem after Joseph told his second dream to his father and brethren. (Genesis 37:12) Notice that Joseph didn't go with the brethren to feed the father's flock. Joseph didn't have such a position of leadership and responsibility to be placed over the flock. So, the brethren could not have thought that Joseph was trying to take their place over the stuff. Okay, it's all about the dream. It's all about a dream that has yet to have any outward signs of manifestation.

It's all about a dream that has yet to have any outward signs of manifestation.

Then, Israel sent Joseph to check on the brethren. Joseph did as his father directed and the brethren were not in Shechem where they were assigned. They were in Dothan. Isn't it funny that folk around you don't do what they have been asked to do and then you are sent to go and check them out? You're sent because you are the one who is trustworthy—the one with the integrity—and you follow instructions. This is why the Dreamgiver showed you a dream where He is going to skip you over all of your brethren, but you must know that they will try to kill you first. Look at Genesis 37:18-20.

> *Verse 18   And when they saw him afar off, even before he came near unto them, they conspired against him to slay him.*
>
> *Verse 19   And they said one to another, Behold this dreamer cometh.*
>
> *Verse 20   Come now therefore, and let us slay him, and cast him into some pit, and we will say, Some evil beast hath devoured him: and we shall see what will become of his dreams.*

Before you have even reached your destination, know that they have already plotted to kill you. They have already assassinated your character and dug your grave. Yeah, the brethren said, "Let us slay him and then throw his dreaming behind into a pit. He won't be dreaming another dream." These boys were outraged because of Joseph's dream. Do you think it's because they knew that there was some truth to it? They knew that they were crooked and couldn't be trusted and they knew that God was also fully aware of these facts.

Learn a lesson from Joseph's brethren. Take note that the Bible says to be anxious for nothing… These guys should not have been anxious, hateful and envious; they got an inheritance.

Let's move forward in God's Holy Word. Turn to Genesis 37:23-24.

Verse 23 And it came to pass, when Joseph was come unto his brethren, that they stripped Joseph out of his coat, his coat of many colours that was on him;

Verse 24 And they took him, and cast him into a pit: and the pit was empty, there was no water in it.

The above scriptures detail the fury of Joseph's brethren. They didn't simply lay hold of him and throw him into the pit, but they stripped him of the coat that his father had given him. The brethren thought that they would remove Joseph's father's covering, but what they didn't realize was that he remained covered by God the Father. God the Father covered him from the crown of his head to the very soles of his feet. They intended to strip him of his anointing, but they didn't give it and they couldn't take it away. The folk desired to take away the dream, but the dream belonged to Joseph and could not be taken away. Has anyone ever tried to take something away from you thinking that its removal would cause you decrease?

The Bible records that after the brethren stripped Joseph of his coat, they *"cast him into a pit, and the pit was empty; there was no water in it."* The Bible was certain to give detail about this pit—this waterless dry pit. Know that the enemy will attempt to cast you down into a pit and create snares for you. He desires to hold you in a dry place and keep you from interacting with the anointing. Although there was no water in the pit, the dreamer still carried the dream. The anointing remained present and not a pit in hell would erase the fact that God had come to Joseph in a dream and spoken visually! Not a pit in hell would stop that dream from coming to pass! God spoke it in a revelatory dream and it shall come to pass! I need to say that again. It shall come to pass!

God Spoke it in a revelatory dream and it shall come to pass!

How many of you know that being cast down into a pit by man is the perfect place for resurrection? God will raise you up over that situation with all power, putting the devil to shame. So, tell Cletus to come on. He might walk over, but he won't even be limping back, because he won't be going back!

Come on now. Follow me. The brethren put the Dreamgiver, the Christ, on the cross. They thought that they could silence His destiny, when in fact nailing Him to the cross sealed His destiny.

Being cast down into a pit by man is the perfect place for resurrection.

That cross was the climatic catalyst responsible for shedding His blood. It was on then, because not even the hollow dry pit, called a tomb could hold Him. Follow me. Follow me. Deep within the tomb, the Resurrection Himself was silent for three days, until His appointed time to wake Himself up, just to have to take a trip to the bowels of hell to get the keys to the kingdom that the devil jacked from the first Adam.

The enemy thinks that he has you wrapped-up in death clothes and buried more than six-feet deep in burdens, but know that your day of resurrection is near. Start counting your three days to dream manifestation! God is so awesome that he allows us to do in three days what would normally take us three-thousand years. One day with the Lord is like one-thousand years. You do the math.

Genesis 37:25-27
Verse 25 And they sat down to eat bread: and they lifted up their eyes and looked, and, behold, a company of Ishmeelites came from Gilead with their camels bearing spices and balm and myrrh, going to carry it down to Egypt.
Verse 26 And Judah said unto his brethren, What profit is it

if we slay our brother, and conceal his blood?

Verse 27 Come, and let us sell him to the Ishmeelites, and let not our hand be upon him; for he is our brother and our flesh. And his brethren were content.

While Joseph is in the pit, his brethren are sitting around eating bread and having a conversation of roast Joseph for dinner.

Know that you are so precious to God that he would deliver up a city for you.

While Joseph suffers affliction at the hands of his brethren, the brethren plot his demise. There are those who set over dinner snikering about your dream, but little do they know that they *"shall be removed"*. (Amos 6:7) Little do they know that *"God will deliver up a city for you."* (Amos 6:8)

Know that you are so precious to God that He would deliver up a city for you. Tell them to come against you if they want. The Lord of Host will come and handle things. They won't even see

It's after you 've been afflicted that you 'll receive the city .

Him. They will just see you looking like Keanu Reeves on the Matrix— doing backbends and flips—just defying gravity with your one-hundred year-old-self. Don't play. You know that leg that you've been talking to everyday, telling it that you are the authority, it will be doing stuff it's never done before. Now, I like that kind of talk. I receive the city, Lord! Do you receive the city? That's what I thought, but know that it's after you've been afflicted that you'll receive the city.

I hope that last statement didn't do too much to your bubble, like burst it. If you have never been afflicted, then THIS IS NOT YOUR WORD! You are simply reading a good book. I'm talking the kind of affliction that put you in a dark place and you questioned whether you'd ever be able to recover! An affliction where you thought that you were going to lose your mind! An affliction where you hung on your cross and cried out, "ABBA Father, why has thou forsaken me!" You want to be raised up? You want to reign? You want to live your dream large? Well, know that you must suffer and you must die. Die to yourself and live unto Christ! If you want to reign with Him, you must suffer with Him! Don't run. It's your destiny.

You must realize that Joseph was a boy with feelings and his brethren tried to kill him! These are his people. He grew up in the same house with these folk. They served on Sundays together. He loved them; he looked up to them and they abused him and desired him dead.

Some might argue, "Don't be so hard on the brethren because the brethren could have killed Joseph, but chose instead to sell him into slavery. Living is better than dying any day." Well, if you read carefully, you would realize that the brethren would have killed him if they could have gained a profit from it. They asked, *"What profit is it if we slay our brother, and conceal his blood?"* I know that you have experienced others trying to kill your dream and sabotage your character just to get closer to someone, to gain a particular platform, or to get a promotion. If you haven't experienced someone trying to kill your dream, just keep living.

Believe me Joseph died the day he was thrown into that pit and sold into slavery. Notice that the scriptures don't even record him speaking as his brothers seized him and dumped his young body into a pit. He never said a word. Don't you see Jesus, here? The Bible records in Matthew 27:12-14 that Jesus "said not a word" when the chief priests and elders afflicted him by accusing him falsely and *"took counsel against Him to put Him to death."* *(Matthew 27:1)* Child of God, when the enemy teams up against you to put you to death say not a word. Know that at that point you are one event away from your crown—from the cross to the crown, from sleep to dream manifestation!

Although Joseph seemed a little immature as we saw him blabbing to the enemy about his dreams, he matured really quickly in a matter of hours. Oh, you don't think that Joseph's silence is a sign

If you haven't experienced someone trying to kill your dream, just keep living.

of maturity? It takes a mature person to remain silent when his brethren are about to crucify him. That is an attribute of an individual who believes the dream and knows where he is really going. It takes a

mature person not to use their rightful God-given office to throw daggers. Who am I talking to? If you are guilty of not holding your peace so that God could get some glory in fulfilling the dream, then you had better repent. If you have held your peace under heavy fire, then you had better shout because your manifested victory is only days away. You may be about to get deported to Egypt, but know that the wealth of the wicked is laid-up for you.

Joseph is about to take an all-expense paid trip to a country with the biggest bank. He is traveling to what was then the capital of the world—Egypt—and is going to make a withdrawal like never before. This withdrawal is going to cover everything and everyone attached to him. When they ask him for his identification, he's going to pull out his *"Suffering Card"*, which will read expires today! Then they will say that he's been positively identified and then they will escort him to the vaults of Egypt to show what he'd just suffered into. Now, you'd better stop belly-aching and give God some praise right where you are!

I'm excited. I'm getting ahead of myself, but I see the end and I like what I see. I want to run!

Genesis 37:28 And there passed by Midianites merchantmen; and they drew and lifted up Joseph out of the pit, and sold Joseph to the Ishmeelites for twenty pieces of silver: and they brought Joseph into Egypt.

Don't be dismayed when your brethren throw you into a dark place and sell you out for twenty pieces of silver. Don't be offended when they seek to destroy your dream and destiny. Although the enemy is trying to smite you, God is trying to get you to a place of rulership and into a position to save nations. What the enemy means for your bad, God means for your good, because everything works together for the good of those who love the Lord and who are called according to His purpose. Know that in your affliction God is trying to take you from the pit to the palace in fulfilling your dreams.

5

Vision in Dark Places:
From the Pit to the Palace—Part Two

The previous chapter demonstrated Joseph's affliction at the hands of his brethren. They greatly afflicted their own brother and sold him into slavery because of his dreams. Remember the dreams entailed ruling and reigning. Let's put the two dreams, recorded in Genesis 37 at verses 7 and 9, before our eyes once again.

> *Verse 7 For, behold we were binding sheaves in the field, and, lo, my sheaf arose, and also stood upright; and, behold, your sheaves stood round about, and made obeisance to my sheaf.*
> *Verse 9 And he dreamed yet another dream, and told it his brethren, and said, Behold, I have dreamed a dream more; and, behold, the sun and the moon and the eleven stars made obeisance to me.*

The *Oxford's Advanced Learner's Dictionary* defines the word obeisance as to show respectful homage or submission to a ruler. Contrary to tradition, the dreams clearly indicated that Joseph would be the one ruling because his sheaf arose and the sun, moon, as well as the eleven stars bowed to him. As a result, we saw that the brethren didn't like it and they determined to kill him. However what the brethren didn't understand was that they were setting Joseph up to rule, thereby making his dreams come true. Understand that you need your enemies. Your enemies are a necessary ingredient in getting God to set the table before you. Your enemies are a necessary element in gaining a foot stool. Although it looked like Joseph was down and out, he was really being set-up to reign and this chapter will detail Joseph's dream manifestation in his ascent from the pit to the palace.

After Joseph was sold to the Ishmeelites for twenty pieces of silver, that foreign nation thereafter sold Joseph *"into Egypt unto Potiphar, an officer of Pharaoh's, and captain of the guard."* *(Genesis 37:36)*

This dreamer of dreams had been despitefully used by his very own brothers and sold into slavery, *yet the Lord was with Joseph.* I can just stay right here all day. The Lord was with Joseph. After he had been scandalized, stripped, disinherited, and pimped, the Lord was still with Joseph! After his dream turned into what seemed to be a nightmare, the Lord was still with Joseph! If the Lord be for you, who can be against you? Let's take a look at Genesis 39:2.

Understand that you need your enemies.

Verse 2 And the lord was with Joseph, and he was a prosperous man; and he was in the house of his master the Egyptian.

Now the Bible says that the Lord was with Joseph. Wait! Wait! Wait! Did the above verse read that the slave, Joseph, was a prosperous man? Indeed it did. So, Joseph the slave being without his crew was a prosperous man. Who made him prosperous? I hope you answered the Lord. Okay, I hear you asking, "Prophet where are you going with this?" Just as the King of Sodom and Gomorrah could never claim to have made Abraham rich, no man can claim to have made Joseph prosperous. It was the Lord who made Joseph prosperous!

Prophetically speaking, child of God, God is allowing you to be in situations where no man can take the credit of making you—where no man can take the credit of making your dream come true. God desires to put so much on you that He has to make sure that no man steals the glory that belongs only to Him. Folk are quick to say, "He is only doing what he is doing because of me." Negro, pleeeeezee! I was already capable of this before you even saw me. As a matter of fact, I was already doing it. I just don't feel a need to make everything public information. Let the Lord tell you who I am. Otherwise, you don't need to know. Folk had better watch themselves and stop being glory thieves and dream stealers.

> *God is allowing you to be in situations where no man can take the credit of making you—where no man can take the credit of making your dream come true.*

Another thing is that when you arrive at the appointed place of rulership and no man can take the credit of getting you there, then you won't have any extra obligations. You can arrive with your integrity intact. You won't owe any favors. You can do things because it is simply the right thing to do and not because your past is pulling your strings. You think that you are free to rule righteously and your past is requesting that you scratch somebody's back who's very capable of giving you fleas!

So, you don't have to take shortcuts. Don't forsake the route of the pit to get to the palace because that is the very route that will apply enough spiritual pressure to push so much anointing out of you that even the heathen will be able to see it. The Bible records in Genesis 39:3 that even Joseph's Egyptian master *"saw that the Lord was with him, and that the Lord made all that he did to prosper in his hands."*

When the Egyptian master, Potiphar, saw this, *"Joseph found grace in his sight" (Genesis 39:4)* and was given an assignment as overseer of Potiphar's house. As a matter of fact, when Joseph was appointed overseer, Potiphar's stuff grew. The word of God records in Genesis 39:5 that *"the Lord blessed the Egyptian's house for Joseph's sake."*

Really digest what is happening here. Joseph has been appointed overseer of a government official's stuff. Ding, Ding! The stage is being set for the dream to come to pass, but know that God will certainly make sure you are prepared before you get to your final place of dream manifestation. This is called training ground. Joseph was first placed over Potiphar's house, while his destiny read Pharaoh's palace! The palace is not merely a beautiful house, but it is symbolic of a place of rulership. It represents the throne of the modern world. Come on into the Spirit realm and stop walking by sight. The Joseph section has taken me somewhere and I am not turning back, not even for you.

Don't despise small beginnings. Although you are where you are now, that place is not your final destination. It's only training ground. If God had sent Joseph directly to the palace from Jacob's house, Joseph probably would not have been able to operate effectively because he had not been trained. Think about it. Joseph's father did not allow him to do anything. When Joseph's brothers were out feeding the flock, Joseph was not with them initially. Joseph was not sent to work, but to check on his brothers. Face it;

Don't despise small beginning.

Joseph, the dreamer was probably babied and untrained. You can be told something all day long, but until you put your hands to it, it is faith without works. We know what that produces—death. Oh, yes it does. The Bible states that *"faith without works is dead." (James 2:20)* Albeit, don't despise your training ground, because it is created to set you up to live your dreams.

As we follow Joseph, we witness that his training ground truly set him up to live his dream. As Joseph conducted Potiphar's affairs, Potiphar himself knew not his own holdings. Genesis 39:6 records, *"And he left all that he had in Joseph's hand; and he knew not aught he had, save the bread which he did eat. And Joseph was a goodly person and wellfavored."* There was none greater in the house than Joseph and nothing was withheld from him but Potiphar's wife. *(Genesis 39:9)*

Know that the thing that you are not allowed to touch is what the enemy will attempt to use as your downfall. We see in Genesis 39:7 that Potiphar's wife lusted after Joseph and commanded him to lie with her. However, Joseph refused daily. *(Genesis 39:10)* The enemy does not have any new tricks. He pulled this one in the Garden of Eden. Yet, instead of touching and tasting, Joseph declined. Joseph's integrity would not allow him to touch the woman. So, she made up a lie and declared to her husband that Joseph had assaulted her and tried to force himself on her. Consequently, Joseph was thrown into prison.

Wait a minute that's another affliction. Joseph is down, but not out. We already know that every time Joseph is afflicted he increases. While he was in prison, the Lord was still with him and he received mercy and favor in that place. When God is with you, you don't die; you multiply.

Stop fretting about where you are. God has proven Himself

faithful to you every step of the way. Yes, the enemy may believe that he has done you in just as Potiphar's lying wife may have believed that she had done Joseph in, but know that whatever you have lost God gave it and He is well-able to restore it. Baby, you are just trading a Pinto for a Bentley and you simply have to supervise people in a dark place for a minute to get it. Oh, did I not mention that Joseph is yet running things in his place of bondage. The prison keeper committed everything to Joseph's hands and the Lord prospered it. *(Genesis 39:22-23)*

While Joseph was serving time for a crime he didn't commit, he encountered two of Pharaoh's chief servants, the chief baker and the chief butler. The two servants had a dream and Joseph interpreted both dreams precisely—the baker was put to death and the butler was restored. *(Genesis 40)* I can't go on without taking a little detour to mention this. Notice that Joseph is being punished for something that he did not do and while he is there suffering he encounters two criminals—one is put to death and one is restored. Does that remind you of anything?

Know that whatever you have lost God gave it and He is well–able to restore it.

Moving on. Joseph's interpretation of the butler's dream declared that the butler would be restored to Pharaoh in three days and Joseph asked that the butler remember him when it occurred. The interpretation was true, but wouldn't you know that the butler didn't remember Joseph until two full years later when a problem arose that no one else could solve. Have you ever done something for someone and they said that they would remember you and they didn't until they needed you again?

Well two years after Joseph had interpreted the butler's dream, there presented a problem that no one in the limelight could solve.

Pharaoh had a dream that the *"magicians of Egypt and all of the wise men thereof" (Genesis 40:8)* could not solve. The Bible goes on to say in that same verse that *"there was none that could interpret the dream."* My God, this sounds like a divine set up. You know that it is, because the butler suddenly remembered the man in the dungeon.

Genesis 40:14-15

Verse 14   Then Pharaoh sent and called Joseph, and they brought him hastily out of the dungeon, and he shaved himself, and changed his raiment, and came in unto Pharaoh.

Verse 15   And Pharaoh said unto Joseph, I have dreamed a dream, and there is none that can interpret it: and I have heard say thee, that thou canst understand a dream to interpret it.

When your appointed time comes, no devil or demon will be able to stop it. You know that Potiphar and his wife were still around. I am sure that they had something to say about Joseph being escorted into the Pharaoh's presence, but not even their story could detour destiny in its set season. You see when your time has arrived you will be brought hastily forward and transformed at the twinkling of an eye. Joseph had to have been covered with grit and grime and somewhat smelly, but he was allowed to clean himself, shave, and change clothes. When you wake–up, there will be no drool, no sticky eyes, no morning breath, and no wild hair. Even when you arrive, you won't look like you suffered anything and your name will precede you before you get there.

> *When your appointed time comes, no devil or demon will be able to stop it.*

Note that when Pharaoh met Joseph he told Joseph that he had heard about his ability to interpret dreams. Stop. Stop. Was Joseph actually interpreting dreams before he left Jacob's house? Was he interpreting dreams at Potiphar's house? When did he start interpreting dreams? He started interpreting dreams in prison. Joseph's gift expanded while he was imprisoned. So, now we see that he is not only a dreamer who has an anointing of prosperity, but that he is an interpreter of dreams as well.

Genesis 41:16 And Joseph answered Pharaoh, saying, It is not in me: God shall give Pharaoh an answer of peace.

Oh, my—my—my! The man is not a glory thief. He will not allow himself to get more attention than God gets. Joseph gives all deference to God concerning his gift of interpreting dreams. Can we please get people to stop taking credit for God's work? Get a revelation that if Jesus be lifted up He will draw all men unto Himself. Therefore if He be lifted up in your vessel He will draw all men unto you, because He lives in you and you in Him. There is no need to stroke yourself. Just stroke Jesus.

Between Genesis 41: 25-32, Joseph interpreted Pharaoh's dream and told him that there would be seven years of plenty and seven years of famine in the land. Then Joseph with the Spirit of Wisdom abiding within him turned around and gave Pharaoh the solution in overcoming the years of famine. Joseph presented a plan to save Pharaoh's kingdom. Don't be mad at Joseph because he seized the moment. As God provides you with divine opportunities, you had better say what the Spirit of the Lord directs you to say. You think that you are going before great men so that they can do something for you, when in fact you are standing before them so that you can do something for them!

When you arrive, you won't look like you suffered anything and your name will precede you before you get there.

God has invested their answer in you. God gave you the dream or the ability to interpret the dream. You hold the answer to save nations. Moreover, you will be made a ruler to accomplish just that.

6

Joseph and a Dream Comes True

In the previous chapter, we witnessed the thirty year-old Joseph interpreting Pharaoh's dream. Know that Joseph was not sent back to the dungeon. He was made second only to Pharaoh. Recall Joseph's dreams. Now let's compare his dreams to what Pharaoh appointed him. Let's read verses 39-44; for, they speak for themselves.

Verse 39 And Pharaoh said unto Joseph, For as much as God hath shown thee all this, there is none so discreet and wise as thou art:

Verse 40 Thou shall be over my house, and according unto thy word shall my people be ruled: only in the throne will I be greater than thou.

Verse 41 And Pharaoh said unto Joseph, See, I have set thee over all the land of Egypt.

Verse 42 And Pharaoh took off his ring from his hand, and put it upon Joseph's hand, and arrayed him in vestures of fine linen, and put a gold chain about his neck;

Verse 43 And he made him to ride in the second chariot which he had; and they cried before him, Bow the knee; and he made him ruler over all the land of Egypt.

Verse 44 And Pharaoh said unto Joseph, I am Pharaoh, and without thee shall no man lift up his hand or foot in all the land of Egypt.

Talk about the vaults of Egypt being opened unto Joseph. All was given unto him. All power was given, except for the power in the throne itself. Joseph ruled Egypt and the people could not lift their hands and feet without Joseph saying so. Was his suffering in vain? I say not! Tell the haters that now you are living your dream and if they choose to step outside of your dream they can, but tell them that they must know they will starve to death if they choose to do that.

Okay, you are saying that you haven't seen where Joseph's family bowed to him. I will briefly cite the remainder of the dream being fulfilled because we already see that Joseph's sheaf did rise from the pit all the way to the palace.

Some may be saying that Egypt is not the whole world so we cannot rightfully say that Joseph saved the world. I believe that Genesis 41:57 will clarify that thought. It reads: *"And all countries came into Egypt to Joseph for to buy corn; because that the famine was so sore in all lands."* In that, we also see that the interpretation was correct.

The word of God said that all of the countries came. Genesis 42 describes that even those in the land of Canaan came. Who was located in Canaan? You have it—the children of Israel. They too came for provision from Joseph. Read the account of *Genesis 42:6.*

Verse 6 And Joseph was the governor over the land, and he it was that sold to all the people of the land: and Joseph's brethren came, and bowed themselves before him with their faces to the earth.

Genesis 43:28
…And they bowed down their heads and did obeisance.

Genesis 44:14
…and they fell before him on the ground

Joseph revealed himself to his family and moved them into Egypt and with Pharaoh's full consent gave them the best part of the land.

It is wise to say that not only were Joseph's dreams fulfilled, but all things were restored back unto him. As with you, child of God, don't be discouraged by your pit stops. Pit stops are merely down time to recoup and energize for the next level. Where your next level is large, know that the circumstances of your pit stops may be extreme, but realize that God is with you and He is for you. Actually Joseph's pit stops were ordained of God as he mentions to his brothers, *"It was not you that sent me hither, but God." (Genesis 45:8)* Again, if God be for you, who can be against you? Look that situation in the face and know that it is only seasonal. It will be gone before the wind changes direction. Be strong and of good courage because God is preparing you to save nations and He is taking you into a land where you will rule and someday leave with all that it has! Know that in your suffering for righteousness sake, God is bringing you into a place where dreams come true.

Don't be discouraged by your pit stops.

SECTION THREE

SOLOMON AND A DREAM COMES TRUE

Difficult Decisions Develop Dreams.
-Dr. Todd M. Hall

Now that you have consumed the dream manifestation of Adam and Joseph, you are invited to partake of *Solomon and a Dream Comes True.* As you are already enthusiastic and energized from the previous sections, the Solomon reading will bring you to a level of excitement which is representative of the erectile state in dream cycles. This state produces an increase in heart rate, a rise in blood pressure, and erections in the male penile area. Don't be afraid. This is perfectly normal. As your body progresses deeper into the sleep cycle your body starts to respond. This response is necessary because you will need to awake sooner or later to make some decisions. Understand that when a dream is of God and it awakes, God will cause you to have to make decisions to develop that dream.

7

Talking in Your Sleep

Let's go to I Kings 3:5 where we see Solomon and God conversing while Solomon is yet asleep.

Verse 5 In Gibeon the Lord appeared to Solomon in a dream by night: and God said, ask what I shall give thee.

The above word of God records that Solomon was having a dream at night. In the dream God spoke to Solomon, the sleeper, asking Solomon what shall He (God) give to Solomon. He asks this because this dream is personal. It is Solomon and God. Some of you go into this type of dream state even when you are awake. When the Lord is really talking to you, you just leave here. Then you return saying, "Oh, I'm sorry. What were you saying?"

God asked, "What shall I give thee?" When did He ask him the question? He asked him while he slept. I guess God has proven in verse 5 that it is hard to reach some of you while you are awake. Many times you have too much to do and too many places to go. You have too many things to handle. So, God determines that He will wait until you go to sleep because that seems to be the only time He can reach you. You do not like that kind of teaching, do you? You want something deeper. It is coming in a minute.

God had to wait until this boy went to sleep. Ask me why. He had to wait because Solomon is a teenager. Solomon is hyper. He is going out, playing and hanging. Therefore the all-knowing God

Many of you have lost friends because you told them what God told you.

waited because He knew that there was purpose in Solomon's life and that Solomon had been anointed to take over some things in his youth, which could not wait until he became older. So, God spoke to the boy king in his dream where it was safe—where he would not go, in his hyper

activity, and tell all of his friends. If he was to tell all of his friends that he is special, that he is the mack, that he is going to control things, then they may not have desired to play with him anymore. Many of you have lost friends because you told them what God told you. You thought that they would rejoice with you, but instead they did a Joseph thing to you and they started disliking you. If they dislike you when you simply tell them that you dreamed your house, then they are going to hate you when you move in. Are you getting this? Then say, "I hear you." I promise you that you will not regret that you read this book.

After God said, "Ask what I shall give thee," Solomon responded. Is he still sleeping? He is surely asleep. Oh, but he is talking. Solomon did not think; he actually said. This is indicated in I Kings 3:6. We are not going to change the Bible.

Verse 6 And Solomon said, Thou hast shewed unto thy servant David my father great mercy, according as he walked before thee in truth, and in righteousness, and in uprightness of heart with thee;

and thou hast kept for him this great kindness, that thou hast given him a son to sit on his throne, as it is this day.

This boy is talking some stuff. Now remember he is asleep; so, you have to put the sleep mode on the words. You cannot talk like you are awake. It is funny how some folk do not really speak their vision or what God is going to do for them until they get tired. They start saying, "I am tired of this. God, you have got to do something about this." Why does it take being tired for folk to begin to speak the words that they should have spoken a long time ago? "I am tired of crying. That is it." You see, it took getting tired. Alright, I think that I had better do it like this. I will only bore you for a couple of more minutes.

If they dislike you when you simply tell that you dreamed your house, then they are gong to hate you when you move in.

To demonstrate this tired notion, let us look at a woman who loves her man, as well as has great endurance and patience concerning her man. If her man is insensitive, abusive or he does not give her props and treats her like she is a child, her love for him will put up with his actions to a certain extent before she begins to say anything about the mistreatment. He will treat her badly and then say, "Baby, I love you." She will continue to look past his actions and reply, "Yeah, I know. I love you too, baby." Then she will walk away. At this point, she is holding everything in. When he does a repeat performance, she will remain quiet and reiterate her love, although her man's actions are really pushing her. She then will go away and get his food. Now when he does it one day in public something inside of her says, "I am tired of this. I need to talk to you. I know that you are the man and you say that you are

You had better start opening your mouth and saying something to the Lord.

anointed. You are the man of God, but do not ever step to me like that again. I may not be a man, but I am a human being and you are going to treat me like one." Now once she gets it all out of her, she sleeps. Most folks that have something on them that they have to get off cannot sleep well. I think that I am boring you.

I Kings 3:7 And now, O Lord my God, thou hast made thy servant king instead of David my father: and I am but a little child...

This verse clearly shows us that Solomon was but a little child. He was but a little sleeping child. Oh, you did not read that, uh?

I Kings 3:8-10
Verse 8 And thy servant is in the midst of thy people which thou hast chosen, a great people, that cannot be numbered nor counted for multitude.
Verse 9 Give therefore thy servant an understanding heart to judge thy people, that I may discern between good and bad: for who is able to judge this thy so great a people?
Verse 10 And the speech pleased the Lord.

Wait a minute. The boy is talking in his sleep. Oh, you still do not like this. He is not awake. So, for everyone who is looking at this strangely, WAKE-UP! He is asleep. Solomon's *speech* pleased the Lord. It does not say that Solomon himself pleased the Lord, his life or his walk, but that his speech pleased the Lord. You may be asking, "So, what does this tell me?" I am glad that you asked. It tells you that you had better start opening your mouth and saying something to the Lord.

8

Watch What You Say in Your Sleep

The previous chapter depicted that you should be talking to God even in your sleep. This chapter will discuss the importance of what you actually say to God.

I Kings 3:11 And God said unto him, because thou hast not asked for thyself long life; neither hast asked riches for thyself, nor hast asked the life of thine enemies; but hast asked for thyself understanding to discern judgment...

We already know that God was pleased with Solomon's speech. Now, look at verse eleven, which tells us what Solomon requested of God. Solomon did not request Nike, Versace, Brione, or DKNY, but he requested of God *understanding to discern judgment.* He did not ask to be a rapper or some big basketball player. Neither did he ask for something restricted to the royal family—no me and mine mentality. The scripture quotes that Solomon did not ask for great riches for himself or for the life of his enemies. Are you reaching in your database and downloading your requests of God? What do you see? Remember that Solomon was prompted by God, the one who holds ownership of the earth and the fullness thereof. God said, "Ask what I shall give thee." Solomon responded that he desired *understanding to discern judgment.* Verse twelve tells us what God did.

Verse 12 Behold I have done according to thy words...

He made a covenant in Solomon's sleep. Yes, a covenant was made in Solomon's sleep. Here, you have two consenting parties (God and Solomon) who have agreed. You will be blessed if you catch this. If you had a dream about a car in your sleep and then awoke and it is not out of you yet, then maybe it is where God *The greatest* made that covenant with you. Maybe after dream-*move of faith* ing about the car you then go about your day and *is in the dark.* that car drives by you. You may say, "That is the same car." Come on and handle the depths of God. Stop believing that God only speaks with you when you are awake. *Faith is the substance of things hoped for and the evidence of things not seen. (Hebrews 11:1)* The greatest move of faith is in the dark. If you can see it, it does not require faith. Why hope for things that are seen? Why would you hope for your paycheck when you have it in your hand every Friday of the month? Well, you know that you do not have enough to drive a Mercedes and pay your mortgage. However, if you go to sleep and see that car or house and awaken unable to shake it, that is God saying, "I do not care about your check." I am simply trying to talk to folk who have had some good dreams. Do not play with me about dreams, because I take that personal. Some of you, especially some African-Americans, are more blessed because a man had a dream. He did not live to see it, but the covenant was made. Now, some of you are living in the reality of that man's dream. They told the dreamer to get back on the plane. They were not afraid of him. They were afraid of his words. I think that I am boring some folks.

I know that God never slumbers nor sleeps, but I am here to tell you that the words that you speak are a result of the dream that you have had or a desire that is innately embedded within you. I

The words that you speak are a result of the dream that you have had or a desire that is innately embedded within you.

am trying not to go there. As seen with Solomon, before you ever qualify your words do. That is why God said, *"Let there be,"* *(Genesis 1:3-14)* and what He said is what manifested. Are you following me? *In the beginning was the word. (John 1:1)* He did not even put Himself first. The Bible records that the *Word was with God and the Word was God. (John 1:1)* The things that you have dreamed will soon have your name on it, whether it is on the title, the deed or the check! Your dream is how God is trying to get you in line. I am going on with I Kings 3:12.

Verse 12   Behold I have done according to thy words…

Isn't that something? God did according to Solomon's words spoken in his sleep. Picture that God is using your mind as his business office. You know that all of the nightmares are about to come. Then the Lord tells all nightmares to "Wait a minute. I am having a meeting. Now when I finish you can do whatever you want to do." Then God steps into your mind, sets up His throne and His computer. He pulls out the contract and His pen with red ink that represents His blood so whatever you dream and whatever He says shall surely come to pass. Then He stays in there with you until you and He come to a solemn agreement while you sleep. You may think that I am crazy, but had you gone to hear Jesus you would have thought that He was more off than I am.

Verse 12   …lo, I have given thee a wise and an understanding heart; so that there was none like thee before thee, neither after thee shall any arise like unto thee.

The devil is upset with some of you. Ask me why. He is upset because when your dreams come to pass there will never be one like you. There are a lot of folks jealous of you because they want to be you. They were not even in your dreams. There are people that I have awakened out of my sleep in the middle of the night

When your dreams come to pass there will never be one like you.

and called to give money to because they were in my dream. I may be asleep and recognize one of the members struggling and I would awake and hear God ask, "What did you dream?" I would reply, "They need food." God would send me to the store to buy the member two of everything and then to take it to the person. God would further direct me to tell them that I know that they may not need this but that I saw them in a dream. Then with tears of joy they tell me that they just told the Lord on the previous night about needing help. When they would tell me the time that they had this conversation with God, it would be the same time that I was asleep. God has made a lot of deals with people in their sleep. If I am boring you then stop reading.

You need to tell Freddie Krueger to get out of your dreams. You know I have wondered why those crazy movies, such as Friday the

You need to tell Freddie Krueger to get out of your dreams.

13th, Halloween, and Poltergist keep coming back. I have determined that all of those demons are allowed to come back to get a role in the sequel only because the starring role has never been cast with someone who has the demon destroying Holy Ghost! They got close with the priest, who had a cross yelling, "Come Out!" Say with me, "I dare them to get somebody speaking in tongues!" You better come on with that. I guarantee you that with a Spirit-Filled, tongue speaking demon buster, there would not have been a part two. I am prophesying now.

There will never be one like you, especially after you get what you dreamed. Right now you are better than certain folk and you do not have anything. When people are jealous of you and you do not even have anything, they know that some-

When people are jealous of you and you do not even have any-thing, they know that something is coming.

thing is coming. What is making certain folk hate you when you are struggling and home alone? You may not even have any financial support and they keep mentioning your name in a negative connotation. People feel this way about you and talk about you because hell has received an announcement that when God wakes you up it will be your time. Know that there will never be another like you. When you wake up and get blessed by final-ly collecting on those things that you dreamed and folk ask you how you got it, tell them that you are just living your dream.

9

More Than You Could Ask or Think

I Kings 3:13 And I have also given thee that which thou hast not asked...

Since you knew how to prioritize relationship over materials, God will give you the material possessions as well. When you seek the kingdom first all the things will be added to you. *(Matthew 6:33)* You do not pray for the things, they are added. So, the reason God is visiting Solomon in his sleep is for a relationship. God did not give him a dream of a car. Oh, do not miss that! He did not give him a dream of a wife. He gave him a dream of Him. What you dream is what you shall receive and what Solomon dreamed was a conversation with God that built a covenant with God. Solomon received all of his material needs because the dream of his walk with God was true. Are you picking it up now? What did Matthew 3:33 say?

The reason God is visiting Solomon in his sleep is for a relationship.

Verse 33 But seek ye first the kingdom of God, and His righteousness; and all these things shall be added unto you.

This verse tells us to seek first the kingdom of God and His righteousness. Then it records that all these things shall be added. Notice that the scripture says, "Shall be added," not might be added, but shall be. So, first you dream your walk with God and every dream that comes after that will be a result of that walk. When you walk with God your dreams never cease. Even after you get one thing, you start dreaming another thing. Although you may already have a car, God wants to give you another one. You may already have a house, but God desires that you have a bigger house. Then, you can lease or sell one. He is trying to set you up. Am I boring you? Do not lie to me. Just close the book if I am boring you. For those of you that I am not boring, return to I Kings 3:13.

> *Verse 13 And I have also given thee that which thou hast not asked, both riches, and honor...*

In other words, God wants to give you money without your losing your integrity, wealth without compromise, riches without having to kiss up to somebody and having to be somebody's flunky. See, some of you readers are not ready for this because you are still jealous of some folk who you think are blessed. Why not trace how they got it? They did not get it right. Some of them had it when they were in sin and they just brought it over. Are you talking to me? The reason some of you are not blessed yet is because God says that when He blesses you, He will do it right. Yes, that is exactly the reason some of you are not blessed, yet. When you get it, you will be able to sleep at night. You will be able to sleep because you will know that you did not do anything outside of the will of God to get it. You will not have a nightmare that you shacked with your baby's daddy to get

When you walk with God your dreams never cease.

your bills paid. God says that He will give you the riches, as well as millions of dollars, but He is going to give it to you with integrity. He is not going to give you six numbers for the lottery. Oh, do not get quiet on that. He is not going to let you dream six numbers! All you have to do is dream the scripture and live it; then when you wake-up all these things shall be added. Do not think that it is funny. You may be asking, "Well, Prophet Hall, are you rich?" Yes, I am. I dreamed it for years before it came. Now case closed!

Let me ask you something before I finish the other verses. If you know that it is God giving you the dream about the cars and the money, why wake-up and talk about the money? Why not talk about the one who brought the dream? The next few statements may get me in trouble. I do not mind the whole world calling and screaming, "Money cometh to me now." However, let me tell you my restrictions. If that money comes and you do not have God, that money is going to send you directly to HELL—do not pass go! What does it profit a man to gain the whole world and lose his soul? *(Mark 8:36)*

Even the money is more intelligent than we are. On the forehead of the dollar, it reads, "In God we trust." It is on the forehead of the dollar. If you attempt to use any United States paper currency and it does not have printed on it "in God we trust," it is a COUNTERFEIT! Some of you are broke now because of the counterfeit, but God is working on a legitimate way. Again when God blesses you, you will be able to hold your head up and say, "This is my car, in my name, without a co-signer." Let me put it like this: good things come to those who wait. Money only has the license to come with integrity—when the person for whom it is coming has been waiting. That means that while you praised Him when you were broke, the money became attracted to you and it came. The money then began to talk to the Lord concerning you. It began to volunteer that the Lord sends it to you. Then you would not need to call on money because money would be on the way. You do not need to talk to money. Talk to God—the owner of all things—and have some integrity.

Unfortunately, nowadays, integrity is a foreign word in the church. Saints desire money and the things without having to go through the process. They want things without having to walk uprightly with some integrity. It is not difficult to be rich. Follow this example of money making with no integrity. If I wanted money to come to me, I know how to take the money I have now, backslide to Miami, buy some drugs, and flip it. It is not hard to be rich. I can take my money and open a little club, put a few hoochie mamas on some tables or the stage, get an alcohol license and be rich. Some of you do not like the truth. You live in the clouds, but your feet are on earth. The reason that you are not as wealthy as you should be and one day shall be is because right now you are casting every Freddy Krueger out of your dreams. Anything that tells you to get it without God's permission is out of the will of God. All of you women could have money if you just do whatever you want to do. The reason that you are broke is that you are waiting on God to make sure that the man is saved and that the man does it right. You could easily get a man to buy you a car or pay your rent. All you have to do is be his woman for sale. All you have to do is fill his ego and say, "You're the man. You're the man." It is not hard to get your needs supplied. It is hard to get your needs supplied when you are doing it right. The use of the word hard, here, means the *weight*. Most folk hate to *wait*.

> *Nowadays integrity is a foreign word in the church.*

I Kings 3:13 …so that there shall not be any among the kings like unto thee all thy days.

Here, the word of God tells you that when you awake from your sleep that what you see on others will not be able to scratch the surface of the things that God has in store for you. Solomon knew all of the kings. The other kings, with their crowns, jewelry, onyx, and sapphire would have nothing on Solomon when he awakes. Close your eyes and get a quick flash of how you would live if tomorrow God gave you everything that you asked. Behold it and then praise Him for ten seconds. Some of you want to move, but you have cement blocks on your feet. You had better break out and move!

> *The reason that you are not as wealthy as you should be and one day shall be is because right now you are casting every Freddy Krueger out of your dreams.*

Verse 14 And if thou wilt walk in my ways, to keep my statues and my commandments, as thy father David did walk, then I will lengthen thy days.

Here is God saying, "If you walk uprightly, keep my word, and do my will, I will let what I give to you live. I will, also, let you live. Your season will, also, be lengthened." Notice that the lengthening comes after walking right; it comes after the covenant. Do not think that because folk have more than you have that they are living right. How long they keep it is determined by how long they have lived right. There are a lot of people who have money and everything, but a few years later they do not have it anymore. They no longer have it because they did not keep the other part of the dream. They ceased to ful-

> *What you see on them will not be able to scratch the surface of the things that God has in store for you.*

fill their part of the covenant.

If you keep your part of the covenant made in your dream, you will live in this blessed season for a long time. I know that I do not want a short blessing. Do not give me a Mercedes for a year and then allow it to be repossessed. You should not want a good man that you brag to all of your friends about and then the next year you are at the divorce court. Give me something where I do not have to say anything because it will speak for me everywhere I go. Some person will say, "That is Prophet Hall's car or that is his wife." Do not even try to step to her because she will rebuke you in the name of Jesus. I want my blessings to speak and I want my *"days to be long upon the land for which the Lord has given me."* *(Deuteronomy 5:16)* I am prophesying now, but some of you are not hearing me. Some of you are missing it! Whoever has been fighting to live right and holding on to get it right, will enjoy their blessings for a long, long time! God says, "For the amount of time you cried, you are going to have the same amount of time to smile and enjoy." Do you really understand what you have just read? You should be running by now! I am going to run right after this.

10

I Kings 3:15 And Solomon awoke and behold it was a dream.

All of this was in Solomon's sleep. He never got up and had a talk with the Lord; he was asleep. He slept through this whole episode. The scripture records, *"And Solomon awoke and behold it was a dream."* It had to be a dream. Ask me why. It had to be a dream because in the dream God said that Solomon should walk upright *"as [his] father David had walked."* (I Kings 3:14) What David is God talking about? Does He mean the David that slept with Bathsheba? *(II Samuel 11:14)* Does He mean the David that ordered Uriah to be on the front line? *(II Samuel 11:15)* Oh, maybe He means the David that was about to go murder Nabal to get Abagail. *(I Samuel 25:34)* What David?

Dreams are inner sources of strength when God is the one painting th picture.

It is strange how we are convicted usually when we are awake. When you are asleep, God shows it to you as it shall be. Many of you have never had a dream where you were crying or repenting. One thing about it is that God is not going to step into your dream and brow beat you when He knows that when you are awake other folk keep doing just that. Why would God continue to do something to you that He knows all day that very thing is being done to you? That is called condemnation, not conviction!

The scripture says that Solomon awoke and behold it was a dream. So, ask yourself, "Am I dreaming or is this really happening?" Did you dream that you are rich or are you really rich? You know when God is talking to you in your sleep, because when you wake-up you walk differently. You may not even have any money at the time, but other folk even notice that you are behaving differently. They may say, "You are acting mighty differently today." Then you respond, "Praise the Lord. God, bless you. I am feeling mighty good today." People who hate you—you know the ones with the demons in them—know that you had a good dream because shortly after they start talking about you. They try to convince you that you need to stop acting like that. They say, "You ain't got nothing. And you ain't never gon' be nothing." Just tell them to talk to the hand, because you know that your dream is real. Dreams are inner sources of strength when God is the one painting the picture.

Verse 15 And Solomon awoke and behold it was a dream.

When Solomon awoke, he knew that he had had a dream. It was the best dream in life. He did not tell anyone, because who would have believed that he had met God in his sleep? He did not tell anybody, because when he woke-up he did not have time to tell the dream. The dream was so the moment he opened his eyes. This is seen in I Kings 3:16-25. God's Holy Word reads:

Verse 16 Then came there two women, that were harlots, unto the king, and stood before him.

Verse 17   And the one woman said, O my Lord, I and this woman dwell in one house; and I was delivered, of a child with her in the house.

Verse 18   And it came to pass the third day after that I was delivered, that this woman was delivered also: and were together; there was no stranger with us in the house, save we two in the house.

Verse 19   And this woman's child died in the night; because she overlaid it.

Verse 20   And she arose at midnight, and took my son from beside me, while thine handmaiden slept, and laid it in her bosom, and laid her dead child on my bosom.

Verse 21   And when I rose in the morning to give my child suck, behold, it was dead: but when I had considered it in the morning, behold it was not my son, which I did bear.

Verse 22   And the other woman said, Nay; but the living is my son, and the dead is thy son. And this said, No; but the dead is thy son, and the living is my son. Thus they spake before the king.

Verse 23   Then said the king, The one saith, This is my son that liveth, and thy son is the dead: and the other saith, Nay; but thy son is the dead, and my son is the living.

Verse 24   And the king said, Bring me a sword. And they brought a sword before the king.

Verse 25   And the king said, Divide the living child in two, and give half to one, and half to the other.

Here, Solomon is faced with a decision that will measure his wisdom. Remember that wisdom is what Solomon requested of God in his dream. We see that there were two harlots who had sons. When they went to sleep, one rolled onto her child smothering and suffocating him. Then she got up and swapped the dead child for the living. After awakening, the mother of the living child had the dead child at her breast and began to breast feed. So, when she pulled the dead child to her breast something in her said,

"This is not mine." When you wake-up and the devil tries to give you something that is not yours, you will know it. You will know that that is not it. You will wake-up tomorrow and know what to get rid of. God says that you will not awaken and accept anything dead, rolled over, squashed, or void of life—just as the woman whose child was the living knew that the dead child did not belong to her.

The woman of the dead and the woman of the living began to debate. The mother of the dead child said, "The living is mine and the dead is yours." The one that gave birth to the living child said, "The dead child is yours and the living child is mine." And all of a sudden they agreed that the only way to resolve the issue was to call for Solomon. Solomon had just awakened and had just asked for wisdom to judge and discern. He is about to find out whether his dream happened overnight. They called for Solomon, the seventeen year old king. They called for the immature, amateur king who had recently cut covenant with God. They called for the one who otherwise would not qualify, having no credit, no job, and no cosigner. They called for the one who would not otherwise be properly positioned to be all that he could be. This is not for those who live off of their checks and they already know how to budget and know what they are going to get in five years because of that check. This is for those who need something now and they do not have five years. They know that they have made mistakes, charging and messing up bills. You know that it is your mistake, but God can make a mistake a miracle if you would only dream!

God says that you will not awaken and accept anything dead, rolled over, squashed, or void of life.

Okay, they brought Solomon, the one who had just said in his sleep that he is but a child and cannot judge. Also, in his dream, he asked for that very ability to judge and God replied that He would give it to him. Now, either way, a situation has arisen to test whether his dream is alive. In order for Solomon to be respected

God can make a mistake a miracle if you would only dream!

as a young teenage king, he must have wisdom. If he would judge this situation in wisdom, he would receive respect and honor. Then Solomon, the one who said that he could not do anything, out of nowhere came up with an answer. He said, "Bring me the living child."

They gave him the living child. He asked, "Whose is the living?" Both women answered, "The living is mine." He further said, "Alright let me hold the living thing." Know that what is being held for you is a lot and alive. It was in the hands of another but He is about to release it to its rightful owner. Seeing someone else

Some of you have suffered too long to accept or hold onto a dead thing.

with what is yours is a nightmare, but when it gets into your hands it is a dream come true. Solomon said, "Give me the living child and a sword that I may divide the living. And this will let me know to whom it belongs." There is no way that a person who does not praise God will

get the living. As for the dead thing, Solomon did not even request to touch it, much less divide it. If it is dead, it is not any good to anyone. Some of you have suffered too long to accept or hold onto a dead thing.

I do not know about you, but I am real. I want all or nothing. That is just my personality. Does anyone else feel that way? When they got ready to divide the child, the real owner said, "Let the child live and let her have it." The other mother said, "Divide it!" There are player haters who really cannot do anything with what is yours, but do not want you to have it either. The player hater's mentality is that he/she does not care what is done with the living as long as it is not given to the dreamer.

Verse 26 Then spake the woman whose the living child was unto the king, for her bowels yearned upon her son, and she said, O my lord, give her the living child, and in no wise slay it. But the other said, Let it be neither mine nor thine, but divide it.

The mother of the living, the Bible says that her bowels yearned. Then she requested that Solomon give the living child to the dead child's mother. At this point, the one who perpetrated no longer wanted the living child to be kept alive or given to her, now that the rightful owner was willing to let the child go. Solomon answered that the child belongs to the one that is willing to walk away. The one who is willing to walk away is the one whose priorities are in order. That person is seeking the kingdom of God more than things—although waiting years to receive. Then when they get it, the Lord asks, "Will you walk away from it to talk to me?" When you put it in the Lord's hands, you must come out on top.

The player hater's mentality is that he/she does not care what is done with the living as long as it is not given to the dreamer.

Verse 27 Then the king answered and said, Give her the living child, and in no wise slay it: she is the mother thereof.

Verse 28 And all Israel heard of the judgment which the king had judged; and they feared the king: for they saw that the wisdom of God was in him, to do judgment.

The above verses instruct us that Solomon commanded that the mother of the living be given back the child and that the child be fully intact, alive and functioning upon the child's return to his mother. That mother was the one who had cried and gone through for the child.

As God declared in the dream, all of Israel heard of Solomon's wisdom. They respected this teenage king because they saw that he had the wisdom to judge and to discern. They saw his dream come true—the dream that he had dreamed just the night before.

Solomon, with his integrity in place, received honor from the people as well as from others in far away places. For example, the Queen of Sheba visited him because she had heard of this King Solomon who possessed such great wisdom. The Queen of Sheba did not send her subjects to Solomon with a message, because what she had heard was so great that it provoked her to take the journey herself. When she saw Solomon's possessions and heard his wisdom for herself, she knew that what she had previously heard could not compare to what she experienced in Solomon's presence first hand. The Queen of Sheba, who had much herself, was so impressed with Solomon's wisdom that she gave him a check of over a million dollars and the cedars of Lebanon. Solomon did not have to spend the money given him on the cedars because the cedars were donated to his kingdom as a gift. This means that when God gives you the money, it will not be needed to buy the thing. The thing will already be there. The money is just to strengthen your position on the planet so that you never will have to live like you did before.

CONCLUSION

A DREAM COMES TRUE

A Dream has no power until the Dream awakes.
-Dr. Todd M. Hall

Now that you have walked the pages of this book and have become enthused, energized, and excited, you should have no problem awaking. You will not awake sluggish as if you were deprived of sleep, because you will have gone through every phase and cycle necessary for the manifestation of the dream. You will awake with the full mobility of every limb and the soundness of mind required to realize and experience your dream come true!

11

Awake Thou That Sleeps

Shake yourself and say, "My dreams are lining me up to get something tangible. No longer will it be locked up inside of me, but when I awake tomorrow, it is going to be looking me in my face. It is going to jump all over me and will let me know who gave it. This time when I dream, I will believe!" Prophesy to yourself, "Sweet dreams!" When you wake-up in the morning, that thing that you dreamed is going to be sweet to you. It is going to be sweeter than the days before, but you had better do what you are supposed to do. You will have to ask yourself, "Am I dreaming or is this really happening?" You may be cool by nature and intelligent, but the Lord says to give Him the glory. When you wake-up, life will not be the same. When you go to sleep tonight, tomorrow a change will come!

There will be folk who think you are crazy. They may look at you and wonder if you have to act like that. You simply tell Freddy Krueger to get out of your dream! You tell Jason to get out of your dream! You tell that nightmare to get out of your dream. You tell the devil that he does not belong in your dream! Get out!@!!!!

However, if you are a radical praiser, then welcome into my dream. If you are not a praiser, you have got to get out of this one. You are like Solomon today. You have enough

When you wake-up, life will not be the same.

wisdom to understand that you do not get your houses or businesses through your college degrees and family's money. When you belong to God, you get these things by doing what Solomon's daddy did. Bless the Lord at all times and *let* His praises continually be in *your* mouth. *(Psalm 34:1)*

You are going to have a nightmare if you do not praise God. I am telling you that the devil knows that God is about to bless you and the devil knows that the blessing is scheduled to arrive soon. So, tonight when you go to sleep, dream where you are going;

You are going to have a nightmare if you do not praise God.

dream how high you are going and when you open your eyes the dream will be a reality. The devil wants you to ignore your dreams. He wants you to believe that your dreams are just fantasy, but when you know God, your dream is

a fantasy that is ready to come to pass. Know that every dream that you had and every vision that you saw, shall come to pass. It shall come to pass! It shall come to pass! Scream!!!

When you wake-up from your dream, everything from that day

Know that every dream that you had and every vision you saw shall come to pass.

forward will be good in your life. No more bad days! Your good days will out-weigh your bad days! Your happy days will outweigh the sad! Weeping may endure for a night, but joy comes in the

morning! Praise God! Praise Him! Praise Him!

The devil will try to tell you that you are foolish to believe that you are going to be rich and for believing that you are healed. He will tell you to snap out of it. Well, you need to let him know that you are out of it. You are out of debt! You are out of Lodebar! You are out of sorrow! Tell the devil that you are going higher!

Your dreams are about to become a reality. Find out who is on your side and just tell them that every dream is about to become a reality. It is all good, because you praised Him when you were going through your hard times. Tell yourself, "Things will get better. This is my last day of being broke. This is the last night of my crying all night long. This is the last night of my being behind. I am on my way. I am on my way higher!"

Adam woke-up and the thing that was in him was out of him. Now he is able to embrace the thing that he used to only be able to feel. You feel rich. Well, picture embracing the manifestation of your richness. You feel that God is going to save your family. You should picture it happening. Being pregnant is like a dream; you know that it is in you, but you cannot wait until it comes out.

Dreams, ambitions, visions and aspirations fall into the same category, because you must wait on all of them to come to pass. There is a dream, vision, or idea incubating inside of you. It is in you because it has plans on coming to pass. God wants you to know that being pregnant is a joy, but giving birth to it is pain, while holding it is pleasure. Some of you all are going through the pain now, but tomorrow will be pleasure. The thing that you cried for is going to now be in your grasp. The crying, pushing, labor and travailing are the steps before the embrace.

Habakkuk 2:3 For the vision is yet for an appointed time, but at the end it shall speak, and not lie: though it tarry, wait for it; because it will surely come, it will not tarry.

If it is tarrying, it is good, because wait is attached to good. Let me modernize it because you think I am crazy, here. Although the vision and dream that you have been having over and over again is taking its precious time, wait for it. It shall speak and not lie. God

Although the vision of the dream that you have been having over and over again is taking its precious time, wait for it.

says to believe in it and it shall come to pass. Do not even tell anyone. They will see it for themselves; the dream will speak, and they will see that you are not lying. I believe in every good dream that I have and I know that without a shadow of a doubt that there is nothing that God cannot do. As ridiculous as my imagination might be, God can do exceedingly, abundantly, above what I can ask or think.

(Ephesians 3:20) So, if I know that I can be a millionaire, He will not have a problem in making me a multi-millionaire. If I know I can get three bedrooms, He will not have any reason not to make me wait another year and just put five on there. The wait increases the dream.

However, you must know that there comes a time when you have to stop dreaming because as long as you continue dreaming you have not awakened. So then, God tells the body of Christ, "Awake thou that sleeps." *(Ephesians 5:14)* It is time to get up. If we read Adam's story properly, it is easily seen that God wakes you up because what is yours is ready. You can wake-up tomorrow with no money and then God shows you where it is. He will show you something that you did not think of. The release is in God's

It is time to get up.

power. He is the alarm clock. When He wakes you up, your life will never be the same. Again, God says. "Awake thou that sleeps." When you get up after dreaming, it will not be through your clock. It is going to be because God says that it is ready. Actually, you need to wake-up like Eve is looking you in your face, like the business is looking you in your face, like the bank loan is looking you in your face, like the finished product of a brand new home is looking you in your face, or like your saved—Holy Ghost filled—children are looking you in your face. Wake-up and embrace what you have dreamed about for so long! This is your wake-up call. Live your dreams!

Author's Biography

Dr. Todd M. Hall is the eldest of nine siblings, born in Brooklyn, New York to a legacy of preachers of the Gospel, including his father, mother and grandparents. Overcoming the lure of the streets to accept his call to ministry has brought this man of God to a number of crossroads. Choosing ministry over fame and fortune has brought him and those who receive his message of purpose in Christ, greater riches.

Dr. Hall is the Founder and Overseer of Shabach Christian Church in Orlando, Florida. He has over 22 years of practical experience as a community leader and youth advocate, which he has used to establish Dove Inner City Ministries outreach to focus on the needs, pressures and concerns of youth. Dr. Hall teaches on real life experiences and biblical principles in a common language understood by youth to persuade them to give their life to Christ. Not only does Dr. Hall reach the youth, but he bridges the gap between the young and the old with one of his most powerful sermons to-date based on the book of Joshua, entitled Sanctified Thug™.

Dr. Hall is internationally recognized as the "Praiseologist" for his wisdom on the application of Praise and Worship and his remarkable skill to locate Praise throughout the entire Bible. One of Dr. Hall's most notable strong suits, is his ability to combine biblical truths and his understanding that the purpose of mans creation is to Praise, and that Worship was created to be an intimate relationship between God and man. Dr. Hall is extremely gifted in the closing delivery of his messages with the melodious sound of his voice and the use of musicians, to bring the anointing of old back into the worship experience.

His excitement and intensity in delivering the Word of the Lord has helped to revive ministries, restore pastors, rebuild churches and renew the hearts and minds of Believers, as well as Non-Believers to a new level of faith and commitment to God.

It is hard to believe when watching Dr. Hall jump, praise and dance to the Glory of God; that several years ago, he suffered a debilitating stroke which left him paralyzed, with partial vision and slurred speech. Through the miraculous healing power of God, Dr. Todd Hall is now using his testimony to impart wisdom and truth to this end time generation.

Once you have experienced the explosive ministry of Dr. Todd Hall, curses will be broken, reversed, and void in your life. You will listen to Dr. Hall with expectation, as he equips your spirit with an encouraging and empowering message to engage in a battle that is already won!

Note to the Reader

The publisher invites you to share your response to the message of this book by writing to Dr. Todd M. Hall in care of Sovereign King's Creation, P.O. Box 161367 Mobile, Alabama 36616, USA. Find us on the internet at HYPERLINK "http://www.sovereignkingscreation.com" www.sovereignkingscreation.com or send an email to: info@sovereignkingscreation.com